Delivering Constructive Criticism

90 Minute Guides

Michelle N. Halsey

Silver City Publications & Training, L.L.C.
P.O. Box 1914
Nampa, ID 83653
https://www.silvercitypublications.com/shop/

ISBN-10: 1-64004-015-3
ISBN-13: 978-1-64004-015-1

Contents

Chapter 1- Constructive Criticism

Constructive criticism can be a helpful tool when used with the intent of helping or improving a situation in the workplace. However, it can be one of the most challenging things not only to receive, but also to give. It can often involve various emotions and feelings, which can make matters delicate. But when management learns effective ways to handle and deliver constructive criticism, employees can not only learn from their mistakes, but even benefit from them.

By the end of this chapter, you will be able to:

- Understand when feedback should take place

- Learn how to prepare and plan to deliver constructive criticism

- Determine the appropriate atmosphere in which it should take place

- Identify the proper steps to be taken during the session

- Know how emotions and certain actions can negatively impact the effects of the session

- Recognize the importance of setting goals and the method used to set them

- Uncover the best techniques for following up with the employee after the session

When Should Feedback Occur?

One aspect of delivering constructive criticism is in knowing the right time and opportunity to deliver it. Some instances can be addressed on the employee's next annual review, while others should be addressed right away. If it is done too soon, it could make the employee doubt their abilities and affect their job performance. If delivered too late, then the employee may ignore it altogether and dismiss any help at all. Identifying key situations can help decide when feedback needs to be done.

Repeated Events or Behavior

An employee that displays repeated negative behaviors or patterns should be addressed in order to either stop or further prevent it in the future. Before addressing the problem, the employee should be monitored to ensure the event or behavior is reoccurring, not a onetime incident. Once it has been identified, the employee should be addressed in private. Privately, a resolution can be found to end the behavior and prevent it from happening further without embarrassing the employee in front of other coworkers.

Examples:

- An employee is constantly tardy to meetings, although they contribute throughout the session.

- An employee turns in their reports in the incorrect format, but they are always on time.

- An employee works hard during the day, but takes long breaks and lunches.

Breaches in Company Policy

Situations such as tardiness, improper dress, and poor performance are examples of a breach in company policy. Problems such as these should not wait until the employee's next review, but should be addressed right away. If not properly handled, the employee's behaviors can start to affect others in the office and disrupt the work flow. Employees should be reminded of the company policy, including guidelines to follow and possible consequences for misconduct.

Examples:

- Excessive tardiness or absences

- Consistent violation of dress code policies

- Disruptive behavior to other employees

- Continued unsatisfactory job performance

When Informal Feedback Has Not Worked

Informal feedback includes actions such as a helpful reminder, a discussion in passing or even an email or memo. Many managers will try one of these methods (or another) to address a problem with an employee and keep the constructive criticism to a minimum. But when informal methods do not work, and the behavior continues the manager needs to then find a form of formal feedback to speak with the employee. Formal feedback, as the name suggests, usually involves a more planned or structured approach, such as a meeting or review. These actions normally allow more direct contact with the employee and can better address the problem, as well as a solution.

Example of formal feedback:

- Private meetings or discussions

- Personal follow-up after a particular incident

- Employee review or appraisal

Immediately After the Occurrence

One of the best times to deliver feedback is immediately after the incident happens. This way, the behavior or problem can be addressed right away. If a problem is ignored and allowed to continue, it can not only affect the employee, but coworkers as well. The longer the behavior goes on or the more time that passes after an incident, the value, and effect of the feedback decreases. Formal or informal feedback can be used, as long as it effectively resolves the problem.

Tips:

- Speak with the employee privately.

- Address the problem – don't criticize the employee.

- Find a solution and how it can be implemented.

Chapter 2 – Preparing and Planning

Management generally finds it easier to deliver any form of constructive criticism once they have prepared what they want to say and how they want to deliver it. The key is to decide what problems or situations you want to address and how you can provide the employee the information they need to succeed. Careful preparation, clear information delivery, and a sense of sensitivity toward the employee will not only result in better employee performance, but possibly a better relationship between management and employees.

Gather Facts on the Issue

Before you can begin to address any situation, you have to gather the facts. It's best to make a quick list of what you'll need to cover and what information you'll need to do that. This can include employee performance stats, memos; emails exchanged, or even notes containing your own personal observations. If needed, include information from company policies or training guides. The more facts and information you gather beforehand, the more prepared you'll be when the time comes meet with the employee.

Hints:

• Review the reason for giving the constructive criticism

• Find what the employee may need to improve or change in the future

• Gather information that supports why you have addressed the problem (i.e. performance stats, behaviors)

Practice Your Tone

The point of constructive criticism is to help the employee and encourage them to improve and be successful. However, the tone of your voice can speak louder than the words you use. If your tone is hard or comes across as disapproving, the employee may interpret the meeting as a form of criticism or discipline and then ignore or dismiss any helpful advice or action plan. On the other hand, if the tone is too light and amicable, the employee may interpret the action plan as friendly advice and not take the need for improvement seriously.

Points to remember:

- Remain neutral – your focus is to help the employee.

- Watch for angry or accusing tones – these can counteract the help being offered.

- Practice what you want to say beforehand. Look for tones and pitches that can either help or harm.

Create an Action Plan

Once the problem has been addressed, an action plan will help the employee to make the proper adjustments and improvements they need. Change can be hard for anyone, so the employee will need proper support from management to succeed. Make realistic goals the employee can achieve and focus on the areas of work the employee has control to change (their duties or department). Once a plan has been made, allow ample time for it to be put in place and monitor the employee to see how they are doing. It may also be helpful to schedule a follow-up meeting to check on their progress.

Tips:

- Give specific feedback and improvements that need to be made.

- Focus on goals the employee can achieve to correct the problem.

- Form an action plan that helps achieve those goals.

- Follow-up as needed.

Keep Written Records

Written and documented records are often important when delivering constructive criticism. Written records not only help track the behavior or actions that need to be corrected, but also help document the actions that will be taken to correct the situation. Document employee behaviors and reactions to keep in employee files and add to the action plan. The action plan can be a form of documentation once it has been written and can also be added to the employee's and manager's work files.

Example of written records:

- Exchanged emails/notes/memos

- Log of employee behaviors or actions

- Action plan with improvement ideas and strategies

- Signed forms signed by the employee (acknowledgement of feedback, actions plan, etc.)

Chapter 3 – Choosing a Time and Place

Choosing a time and a place to deliver constructive criticism can play a key role. The location should allow for the parties to speak in private and away from other coworkers. Many factors can affect what would be the best time, such as if the employee is tired or getting ready to go to lunch. Also the manager should consider how they are feeling before setting a time. If they are angry or uncomfortable with the subject, they may need more time to prepare.

Check the Ego at the Door

One of the first steps in delivering constructive criticism is to remove the emotions involved. This includes the manager's emotions and the possible ego they can bring with them. When preparing to speak with an employee, leave opinions and emotions at the door and deal with the subject at hand. Don't let something such as your personal opinion of the employee or your knowledge of the subject affects how you resolve the problem.

Tips:

- Focus on the issue, not the person.

- Remain open to suggestions or questions.

- Don't harp on an issue. Say what has to be said and move on.

Criticize in Private, Praise in Public

Constructive criticism shouldn't be done in a public setting, such as the employee's cubicle or the break room. Confronting an employee in front of coworkers or in a common area can cause embarrassment or anger, which counteracts the purpose of offering help and creating solutions. A private meeting allows both parties to speak and go over every aspect of the issue. The employee can feel free to ask questions and not feel as though they are being attacked in a group setting.

Ensuring that the conversation takes place in private and only between the relevant parties not only eliminates unnecessary gossip, but shows respect for the employee and their future success. On the other hand, praising the employee in a public setting can not only boost morale for the employee being praised, but also for all employees who witness it. This allows employees to see firsthand that the company they work for not only discusses changes that must be made with employees, but also appreciates the things that employees are doing right!

It Has to Be Face to Face

When delivering constructive criticism, the best method is always to speak face to face with the employee or other parties. Even though we live in the electronic age and rely on technology too often communicate with others, a traditional face to face meeting is always best when delivering news or criticism to someone. Emails or written letters are usually one sided and portray accidental tones. Phone calls can cause intimidation and usually do not allow the employee to speak in private if the phone call is made on an office phone. Speaking with the employee live and in person leaves no room for implied tones or pressures and allows them to speak openly. After the initial meeting, it is acceptable to follow up in an informal method, such as email or phone call.

When meeting face to face:

- Meet in a private setting where everyone can be comfortable.

- Keep a respectable distance, but remain close enough to speak without raising your voice.

- Speak directly with the employee and turn your focus to them when they are speaking.

Create a Safe Atmosphere

The last thing an employee wants to feel is that the manager's office is a place of discipline or criticism. Don't make employees fear coming into your office. Establish trust and open communication with your employees and ensure them that you are available to them. Ensure employees that they can approach you with any questions or concerns they may have. This allows you to create a safe atmosphere and environment where you can deliver the constructive criticism you need without making employees feel as though they are in a torture chamber.

Benefits of a safe atmosphere:

- Employees are more open to approaching you with problems or concerns.

- Allows you to deliver news or criticism to employees without frightening them.

- Employees feel more at ease hearing constructive criticism.

Chapter 4 – During the Session

After thoroughly preparing the information and process needed, the manager is ready to successfully deliver the needed constructive criticism. Remain businesslike and focus on the problem at hand. After both parties have had a chance to speak and express their position, both parties can move toward the corrective action and solution.

The Feedback Sandwich

The purpose of the feedback sandwich is to offer coaching and support while softening the blow of the initial criticism. It's referred to as a 'sandwich' because the manager should start with a compliment before introducing the criticism. Then follow up with another positive statement. This technique allows the employee to hear the necessary criticism, but also gets to hear the good points of their performance too. The feedback sandwich can be an effective tool to use, but if used in excess or without sincerity, the compliment process can seem cheesy and employees may only focus on the negative.

Step to the Feedback Sandwich:

- Prepare and outline what you want to say or address

- Identify the positive and make a compliment

- Present the criticism and facts

- Add another positive statement and encouragement

- Follow up with the employee periodically

Monitor Body Language

Body language can be a good indicator of how someone is feeling and how they are accepting what is being said. When the manager is speaking, gestures such as furrowed brows, eye rolling, or certain standing positions can make the employee feel uncomfortable and dismiss what is being said. The manager should not only monitor their own body language, but pay attention to gestures the employee may be making, such as squirming in their seat, fidgeting, or not making eye contact. Based on the employee's body language, the manager may need to change tactics and approach the subject in a different way.

Common body language gestures:

- Eye rolling

- Fidgeting

- Looking away or not making eye contact

- Certain stances, such as leaning away, slumped shoulders, or crossed arms

Check for Understanding

After the manager has delivered the constructive criticism and is preparing to put the action plan into play, they must check for understanding from the employee. Allow the employee to ask questions and add input to the solution. Ensure that the criticism is understood clearly and that it is meant to help the employee grow and succeed, not to single them out or make them feel like a target. Reassure the feedback is for their benefit and that they understand the information is provided to make positive changes in the future.

Practice Active Listening

Active listening is where a person makes a conscious effort to hear what the other person is saying. This requires your full attention, so try to ignore distracting noises or situations around you. Don't dwell on responses or answers you want to make when the person stops speaking, as this can take your attention away from the message. Some tips you can include are saying the other person's words back to yourself and using body gestures such as head nodding to acknowledge what is being said. When they are finished, follow up with questions or comments to show you've taken in the information.

Keys to active listening:

- Pay attention to the speaker. Try not to let your mind wander.

- Show you are listening by using body language, such as nodding your head or smiling.

- Provide feedback and ask questions.

- Allow the speaker to finish talking. Don't interrupt with counter arguments.

- Respond respectfully and offer opinions or comments.

The end of the session is the key part that allows the manager and the employee to come together to make a plan of improvement or change. If the action plan is only made by one party, the terms can be one-sided and won't address the roles in which both parties need to take. While this can be a delicate subject to approach, with the correct planning and outline, a plan can be formed and implemented in no time.

Set Goals

When creating an action plan, one of the most important steps is to create goals to help the employee improve or make changes. Ask the employee what they want to accomplish and find ways to work together in reaching these goals. Set goals that are realistic and can be achieved by the employee in a reasonable amount of time. Then outline a plan and a sample timeline depicting what actions should be taken to achieve these goals. Offer ways you can help the employee reach these goals.

Common goals managers and employees make:

- Improve training or skill sets

- Decrease absences or tardiness

- Increase general job performance

- Reduce errors and future mistakes on trouble areas

Be Collaborative

Working together to correct a problem not only helps make the appropriate changes, but it can strengthen the team bond between the manager and employee. Knowing they will always have support from management encourages employees to work harder and come to you sooner rather than later if they have a problem. Allowing employees to be a part of the solution will make them feel as though they are contributing and will feel more willing to make the necessary changes and improvements.

Tips:

- Make sure you and the employee realize what needs to change or improve.

- Address what actions should be taken to achieve these changes.

- Ask the employee for input and what actions they can take to help.

- Form a plan together that both parties can agree to.

Ask for a Self-Assessment

One of the more difficult parts of delivering constructive criticism is asking the employee to perform a self-assessment. While the manager may have plenty of comments or opinions about the employee and their performance, a self-assessment may seem like a graded paper the teacher gives in school. Employees are more likely to recognize their own mistakes when they are not just being *told* to recognize them, but that they can *see* it for themselves. Ask the employee to take the time to analyze their skills and abilities and what actions they have recently taken. By forming skillful questions the employee can think over not only what helps them recognize their mistakes, but also perceive the criticism as a means to benefit their growth as a worker. Once they have finished their self-assessment, they are not only ready to own up to their shortcomings, but they are more willing to learn from them.

Always Keep Emotions in Check

After you've checked your ego at the door, be sure to check on your emotions also. To effectively deliver constructive criticism, you must eliminate any personal emotions or feelings. Emotions can make you susceptible to bias and can make what you have to say seem one-sided or narrow-minded. View the situation from a business-like point of view. To a certain extent, the employee's feelings should be taken into consideration when delivering the information. You might not be able to save them from a little embarrassment, but outright humiliation can and should be avoided.

Tips:

- Consider the employee's feelings (put yourself in their shoes)

- Don't confuse the employee with the mistake

- If you are feeling angry or upset before confronting the employee, take additional time to think it over and calm yourself

Chapter 5 – Setting Goals

Now that you are ready to put your action plan into play, together you and the employee need to set goals that can be achieved to improve the employee's future performance. What kind of goals should both of you set? What areas should be included? These are some of the questions you can face when planning goals, and knowing how to outline their future path with the employee will ensure you'll be able to effectively answer them when the time comes.

SMART Goals

Goals are usually one of the most valuable tools when planning success, but they are often not used to their full potential. Goals that are created to help the employee achieve and be successful are often referred to as S.M.A.R.T. goals. S.M.A.R.T. goals are used to outline what steps should be taken and how to follow through with it. Employee success rates are generally higher with these goal plans since they are specific to the individual person.

The five steps to outlining S.M.A.R.T. goals are:

SPECIFIC: In order for you to achieve a goal, you must be very clear about what exactly you want. Often creating a list of benefits that the accomplishment of your goal will bring to your life, will you give your mind a compelling reason to pursue that goal.

MEASURABLE: It's crucial for goal achievement that you are able to track your progress towards your goal. That's why all goals need some form of objective measuring system so that you can stay on track and become motivated when you enjoy the sweet taste of quantifiable progress.

ACHIEVABLE: Setting big goals is great, but setting unrealistic goals will just de-motivate you. A good goal is one that challenges, but is not so unrealistic that you have virtually no chance of accomplishing it.

RELEVANT: Before you even set goals, it's a good idea to sit down and define your core values and your life purpose because it's these tools which ultimately decide how and what goals you choose for your life. Goals, in and of themselves, do not provide any happiness.

TIMED: Without setting deadlines for your goals, you have no real compelling reason or motivation to start working on them. By setting a deadline, your subconscious mind begins to work on that goal, night and day, to bring you closer to achievement.

The Three P's

Goals can't be achieved over night; they take time to plan, make reviews, and then take action. The Three P's are helpful tools that aide you and your employee in achieving goals that you've prepared together. Each step of the Three P's, purpose, planning and partnering, can help you manage and strive toward your goals by outlining key steps, and tips to remember.

The Three P's:

Purpose: Decide what the purpose is of your goal. Do you want to improve job performance? Maybe decrease errors? The purpose of your goal is what you are willing to work for and go after.

Planning: Outline your goals and the steps needed to achieve them. Long term goals can be broken down into smaller, short term goals to make the process easier.

Partnering: No matter how self-disciplined you perceive yourself, it is always best to seek help when planning and pursuing your goals. Get support from your coworkers and management. Don't be afraid to rely on others for help.

Ask for Their Input

Setting goals is not a one way street when working with another employee. Both parties should know the purpose of the goal and realize what efforts will need to be made to accomplish them. If one person decides on the terms of a goal, it may come across as an order or demand rather than a mutual plan. As a manager, let the employee know what you want to see in regards to achievements and accomplishments, but also ask them what they want to gain from it. Have them input ideas and plans they feel will help them succeed. Ask them to come up with things they can do to achieve their goals and then ask what you can do to be a part of it. When goals are made as a team effort and the employee feels they have your support, they will be more willing to work for it and succeed.

Be as Specific as Possible

Goals that are specific and precise will work better than goals that are generalized and vague. For example, when planning goals with an employee, the phrase "I'd like to see you do better on your reports each week" doesn't specify a purpose or needed action. Instead, something such as "I'd like to see you improve your editing and proofreading skills before you turn in your next report" expresses a specific action that needs to be taken, and a tentative time line. Goals sound more 'doable' when they outline what specifically needs to change and improve. When they are presented with unspecific needs or information, they can seem like a guessing game.

Tips:

Name a specific action or topic that needs work

If you have multiple topics, break them up individually. Accomplishing three smaller tasks is easier than one large one.

If possible, give a time line in which actions should be done. Remember to be flexible.

Chapter 6 – Diffusing Anger or Negative Emotions

Unfortunately, constructive criticism is often accompanied by some form of anger or negative emotion, such as denial or embarrassment. The goal of constructive criticism is to help the employee grow and improve, not to hurt their feelings or downplay their work. Therefore, it should be delivered in the correct manner and without negative undertones. When criticism is delivered correctly, emotions can generally be set aside and both parties can focus on the issue.

Choose the Correct Words

Much like our tones, our words can send the wrong message when used in the wrong context. Words that can portray blame or negative criticism are generally rebuffed and can create someone to become defensive. Avoid the 'you messages' that place the blame or problems on the other person. Start sentences with "I" and express how their actions affect you and the company, rather than just criticizing their behavior. The correct phrasing can make all the difference when trying to deliver sensitive constructive criticism.

Incorrect vs. correct word examples:

- Don't start a sentence with "you"; begin with "I"

- Avoid words such as "angry", "outraged," or "furious"; words such as "confused" or "disheartened" will help to keep the mood calmer.

- Express understanding rather than fury or disbelief.

Stay on Topic

Sometimes we can have a lot of ideas and topics going through our head at once, or we try to multi-task between different areas, which can ultimately make us lose focus on what is important. When delivering constructive criticism, it is important to stay focused and stay on topic. Keep eye contact with the employee and avoid trying to do tasks on the computer or fiddle with paperwork. Deliver one topic at a time and completely finish with it before moving on to the next one. Trying to combine several topics into one speech can overload the employee and make them miss the main points. Also, be sure to leave past occurrences in the past. Bringing up problems from the past can distract from recent mistakes and can confuse the employee as to what he's supposed to be talking about today.

Tips:

- Avoid words such as "however", "although", and "but" since they can lead to other thoughts and topics.

- Keep eye contact with the employee. This will help you to focus on them and the issue at hand.

- When speaking with the employee, stop any previous task you were working on. Do not try to combine them.

Empathize

Before a manager can even begin to deliver constructive criticism to an employee, they must first stop and put themselves in the employee's shoes. Remember what it was like to be in their place? Remember how vulnerable and defensive you felt? Think of how the employee would respond to what you have to say. Help your employee feel at ease by empathizing with them and letting them know you are there to help. Criticism that is delivered with empathy in mind is more likely to be accepted by the employee and can even strengthen business relationships.

Try to Avoid "You Messages"

When we're angry or upset, our self-defense mode normally wants to find blame somewhere else, or on "you". This is especially common when trying to deliver constructive criticism. Phrases such as *"You were late yesterday"* or *"Your poor attitude is affecting everyone"* can appear unprofessional and make it appear as though you are insulting the employee. Instead, focus on how it makes others feel, such as *"I felt disappointed when you were late yesterday because we went over some important topics in the meeting"* or *"Our customers were very upset when you greeted them in an unfriendly manner."* The employee will begin to see that you are trying to portray how their actions affect others instead of feeling as though you are blaming or attacking him.

Common "You messages" to try to avoid:

- *"Your job performance has been lagging lately."*

- *"You've been late every day for the past week."*

- *"Your disruptive behavior is starting to affect your coworkers."*

- *"You've been slacking off on your duties."*

Chapter 7 – What Not to Do

There are always helpful tips for what you're supposed to do when delivering constructive criticism, but there are often times that people don't tell us what we *shouldn't* say. Managers can learn all the right things to say and feel they may have everything they need, but knowing what sensitive topics and negative phrases to avoid can be just as crucial.

Attacking or Blaming

Constructive criticism is meant to attack the problem at hand, not the person. Blaming or attacking the employee doesn't resolve the issue, but can actually make matters worse. This can cause the employee to become defensive or even resentful, which in turn makes them lose their trust and respect for you as well as their job. When addressing the employee, remove thoughts of blame or personal attacks and focus on the actual problem at hand. Even though the employee has made a mistake, that doesn't mean they *are* the mistake or that it is a reflection on their character.

Tips:

- Avoid starting sentences with "You" – these sentences always end in blame.

- Separate the problem from the person – i.e. being tardy doesn't mean the person is lazy.

- Avoid words with negative connotations, such as "angry", "frustrated", or "disbelief".

Not Giving Them a Chance to Speak

Generally, people have an inner need to be heard and feel as though others understand their point of view. If a person (or employee), feels as though this need is not met, they can become angry and resentful. Arguments can start since both parties try to talk at the same time, hoping to make the other one listen to them. One simple way to avoid this complication is by allowing the employee a chance to discuss the issue and add their input. After you speak, give them a chance to respond without interrupting. Be open to hear their opinions and concerns as well.

Tips:

- Allow time for one person at a time to talk uninterrupted for several minutes.

- Let the employee know they can express whatever they are feeling, positive or negative.

- Keep an open mind to receive the employee's feedback as well.

Talking Down

When delivering constructive criticism, it is important not to let the tone of the conversation become derogatory, or 'talking down'. Talking down not only insults the employee, but it dehumanizes them and makes you forget you are talking to a real live person. Using angry words or attaching a character label to the employee, such as jerk or idiot, will only put the employee on their defense and create arguments and conflicts. As a manager, when you are speaking with an employee, keep in mind that there is a person in that chair and that they deserve to be treated with respect. They are there for you to unleash your anger or frustrations on.

Remember:

- Avoid attaching character labels or name calling.

- Be aware of the tone of voice you are using – how do you sound to others?

- Approach the employee using a one-on-one level – treat them as your equal.

Becoming Emotional

If your emotions tend to control your actions or responses, then take a few extra minutes to review the situation before delivering constructive criticism. These emotions can make it seem too easy to unleash on the employee and you may not be able to restrain yourself. Becoming emotional can not only make you seem unstable or bias, but it upsets the employee and can make them try to become emotional in retaliation. Before you can begin to address another employee's behavior, you need to step back and take a few minutes to gain your composure and focus on the topic at hand. Going into a meeting with your emotions fully loaded will not get you the results you need.

Helpful hints:

- Avoid trying to personally attack the employee.

- Do not let emotions control the mood in the room – yours or the employee's.

- Plan ahead – decide what you want to say and ensure that you've gained your full composure.

Chapter 8 – After the Session

Constructive criticism should not be done without a proper follow-up. Schedule some sort of follow-up meeting to check on the employee's progress and see if they have any additional questions or concerns. Make yourself available to the employee and let them know how they are doing. If goals were met and the employee has improved, congratulate them. If not, go back to the drawing board and see what other actions need to be taken. Don't leave the employee in the dark about their progress or shortcomings.

Set a Follow-Up Meeting

Follow-up meetings are important in letting an employee know how they are doing after you last spoke with them and created an action plan together. Review the employee's performance stats and determine if things have improved or if the action plan needs to be remade. Feel free to praise positive achievements in public, but remember to provide any additional constructive criticism in private.

Remember:

- Once a follow-up meeting has been scheduled, keep the appointment.

- Praise the employee in public, but give criticism in a private meeting.

- Encourage the employee to keep up the good work

Make Yourself Available

Once the employee is given the action plan and sent back out to the workplace, it is important to let them know they are not alone in their journey. Assure the employee your door is always open and that they are free to approach you with any questions or concerns. Periodically check in with the employee to see if you can be of any help. They may not need you at the moment, but they'll appreciate the gesture and know that you are there to help when they do.

Tips:

- Be open to listen to the employee and their needs.

- Maintain an open door policy – make sure your employees are aware of it.

- Always be approachable – remain interested in your employees and avoid becoming too distant.

Be Very Specific with the Instructions

When creating an action plan or setting up goals, instructions need to be specific and action-oriented. Vague instructions such as "Do better on the next report" don't address the problem, corrective action, or possible timeline needed. A better response would sound something like *"I'd like to see you improve your proofreading skills before you complete your next report"*, which not only provides a specific problem that needs to be corrected, but gives a tentative time in which it needs to be completed. Let the employee know exactly what needs to change and ways to make it happen. General or vague instructions can often be misinterpreted and can cause the employee to exhibit regression rather than progression.

Specific instructions include:

- A set problem to be fixed or corrected.

- Steps or actions that should be taken.

- A possible timeline in which the task should be completed.

Provide Support and Resources

As part of making yourself available to the employee, also make available any additional support or resources they may need, such as other managers or training resources. As a good manager, don't forget to offer plenty of encouragement and personal support. An action plan would not be able to succeed if the employee does not have the support and resources needed to work it. Ensure the employee can always use you as a resource and if they need something they cannot find or get on their own, you will do your best to provide it to them.

Example of additional support and resources:

- Emotional support and encouragement

- Coworker and other management support teams

- Additional training times and materials

- Additional reading material – including manuals, brochures, pamphlets.

One of the most important business tools is being able to provide feedback and constructive criticism to your employees. As a manager, part of your job is to ensure every employee performs to their highest potential. You provide guidance, feedback and the occasional criticism to help them succeed and continue to improve. Don't lose sight of the reason for giving constructive criticism – which is to help the employee grow. After the session, don't lose focus of what you set out to accomplish together. Remember the action plan, the goals set and don't forget to follow up!

Focus on the Future

Past event and past performances are just that – in the past. One of the points of constructive criticism is to move forward and look to the future for improvements. Focus on what can be done or be changed now, rather than what did or didn't happen before now. This is the time for you and the employee to create a plan of action and potential goals the employee can do to change what is currently wrong. Plan on future strategies that are solution oriented. Forget what may have happened before and look toward a better tomorrow.

Measuring Results

When conducting a follow up session, decide how improvement and growth should be measured. Based upon the tasks being completed, different forms of evaluations can be done. Decide what task your employee was in charge of doing and review what they were supposed to be working on. In many cases, written evaluations can be helpful, but sometimes managers choose to drop in and witness the employee at work. However you decide to complete it, the employee deserves to have their results and progress re-evaluated periodically and told how they are measuring up.

Sample ways of measuring results:

- 'Secret Shopper' surveys

- Personal, one-on-one meetings

- Written evaluations or reviews

- Personal monitoring and observance

Was the Action Plan Followed?

Think back on what action plan you and the employee decided upon. Review the tasks that were outlined together, as well as goals and objectives that were set. Analyze if the employee is on track with the plan and what tasks they completed at a certain point in time. Did they follow the plan or stray from it? Did they maintain their timeline goals? Are they showing improvement that would come with completion of the action plan? These are all points that should be evaluated before confronting the employee directly. Once you have had a chance to review their progress on your own, schedule a follow up meeting and see if and where they are having trouble meeting their goals. Discuss any roadblocks they may have hit or resources they can use to get back on track.

Points of the action plan to review for improvement:

- What plan of action was decided upon?

- What goals were set?

- What specific tasks were outlined for improvement?

- Was there a timeline in place? Was it reasonable?

If Improvement is Not Seen, Then What?

After the employee has had time to work their action plan and you've held a follow-up meeting, what do you do when you find there hasn't been any improvement? First, the manager and employee should attempt to rework or rethink their action and goal plans. Do corrections or alteration need to be made? Does the employee need a different course of action? As a manager, provide additional training and support (previously mentioned) to give the employee an extra boost. Ask what you can do to help them be more successful. After a new plan of action has been made, release the employee out on their own again. Let them know you will meet on a regular basis to review their progress and how they are doing on the job.

Helpful tips:

- Identify several areas that are lacking improvement and how that can be changed.

- Provide additional support and opportunities.

- As a last resort, outline the possible consequences for a lack of improvement over time.

Additional Titles

The 90 Minute Guide series of books covers a variety of general business skills and are intended to be completed in 90 minutes or less. It is an effective way for building your skill set and can be used to acquire professional development units needed by project managers and other industries to maintain their certification. For the availability of titles please see

https://www.silvercitypublications.com/shop/.

No. 1 - Appreciative Inquiry

No. 2 - Assertiveness and Self Control

No. 3 - Attention Management

No. 4 - Body Language Basics

No. 5 - Business Acumen

No. 6 - Business and Etiquette

No. 7 - Change Management

No. 8 - Coaching and Mentoring

No. 9 - Communications Strategies

No. 10 - Conflict Resolution

No. 11 - Creative Problem Solving

No. 12 - Delivering Constructive Criticism

No. 13 - Developing Creativity

No. 14 - Developing Emotional Intelligence

No. 15 - Developing Interpersonal Skills

No. 16 - Developing Social Intelligence

No. 17 - Employee Motivation

No. 18 - Facilitation Skills

No. 19 - Goal Setting and Getting Things Done

No. 20 - Knowledge Management Fundamentals

No. 21 - Leadership and Influence

No. 22 - Lean Process and Six Sigma Basics

No. 23 - Managing Anger

No. 24 - Meeting Management

No. 25 - Negotiation Skills

No. 26 - Networking Inside a Company

No. 27 - Networking Outside a Company

No. 28 - Office Politics for Managers

No. 29 - Organizational Skills

No. 30 - Performance Management

No. 31 - Presentation Skills

No. 32 - Public Speaking

No. 33 - Servant Leadership

No. 34 - Team Building for Management

No. 35 - Team Work and Team Building

No. 36 - Time Management

No. 37 - Top 10 Soft Skills You Need

No. 38 - Virtual Team Building and Management

* 9 7 8 1 6 4 0 0 4 0 1 5 1 *